Paul Dukas
"THE SORCERER'S APPRENTICE"

and

Emmanuel Chabrier
"ESPAÑA"

in Full Score

DOVER PUBLICATIONS, INC.
Mineola, New York

-

Bibliographical Note

This Dover edition, first published in 1997, is a new compilation of two works originally published separately. *Paul Dukas / L'Apprenti sorcier / Scherzo d'après une ballade de Goethe
(1897)* was originally published by Durand et Fils, Paris, n.d. *España / Rapsodie pour
Orchestre / Emmanuel Chabrier* was originally published by Enoch & Cie, Paris, n.d. [1883].
Goethe's text originally appeared in the Durand score in a French translation by Henri
Blaze. Dover's English translation is by William Gibson, from *The Poems of Goethe . . . Done
into English Verse,* published by Henry Holt and Company, New York, 1886.

International Standard Book Number: 0-486-29826-4

Manufactured in the United States of America
Dover Publications, Inc., 31 East 2nd Street, Mineola, N.Y. 11501

CONTENTS

French Terms in the Scores

à, to, at
assez en dehors, somewhat to the fore
assez lent, rather slow
assez marqué, somewhat accented
avec (la) bag(uette), [struck] with the stick, beater
avec (la) sourdine = con sordino
avec le bois = col legno
avec le tampon, [strike the cymbal] with
    the cotton-tipped beater

bag(uette)[d'] éponge, sponge-tipped beater
bag(uette) de bois, wooden beater
bien chanté = molto cantabile
bien marqué = ben marcato
bouché(s), stopped [brass]

corde(s), string(s)
cuivrez les sons, make brassy sounds

de, of
détaché, detached
doux et très lié = dolce e molto legato
du talon, at the heel [of the bow]

en animant (un peu) (toujours), becoming
    (somewhat)(continuously) livelier
enlevez la sourdine, take off the mute
en mesure = a tempo
en retenant un peu = poco ritardando
en serrant = stringendo
et, and
étouffez le son, choke the sound

la, le, les, the
laissez vibrer, let ring
léger (et détaché) (et gracieux), light
    (and detached) (and gracious)
les deux, both
lointain, distant

mais, but
mouvement (mouv^t) = tempo
    au mouv^t = a tempo
    1er mouv^t = Tempo I
montez le Fa grave au Lab, raise low F to Ab
    [timpani]

ôtez les sourdines, remove the mutes
ouvert(s), open [brass]

plus animé, livelier
plus retenu = più ritardando
posit(ion) ord(inaire), [play] in the usual way
prenez les sourdines, put on the mutes
près de la table, near the sounding board [harp]
près du chevalet, near the bridge [strings]

retenu = ritardando
revenez au mouv^t initial, return to the first tempo
roulement avec une double mailloche, roll with a
    two-headed bass drum stick

sans bag(uette), [cymbals struck] without the stick
sans presser, unhurried
sans sourdines = senza sordini
sec, dry, very short
serrez (un peu) (peu à peu) le mouv^t, hold back
    the tempo (a little) (little by little)
sons d'écho—prenez le doigté un 1/2 ton au dessus,
    echo effect: finger the pitches a half-step
    higher [brass]
sons ordin(aires), actual pitches
sur le chevalet, on the bridge [strings]

talon de l'archet, heel of the bow
toujours = sempre
toujours plus animé, increasingly lively
tous = tutti
très = molto
très doux, very gentle
très en dehors, strongly to the fore
très légèrement retenu, very lightly held back
très marqué = molto marcato
très vif = molto vivace

*une cymb(ale) suspendue par sa courroie: roulement
    avec deux bag(uettes) d'éponge*, one cymbal
    suspended by its strap: [play the] roll with
    two sponge-tipped beaters
unies = unisono
un peu en dehors, slightly to the fore

velouté et très léger, velvety and very light
vif, lively

Paul Dukas
THE SORCERER'S APPRENTICE
Scherzo after a Goethe ballad

[L'Apprenti sorcier: Scherzo d'après une ballade de Goethe]

(1897)

Gone is my old wizard master,
  Gone at last—a chance uncommon!
There can happen no disaster
  If his spirits I should summon.
Of the words and motions
  In his necromancy
I've the clearest notions—
  I will please my fancy.
      Boil and bubble!
      Water sources!
      Water courses!
      Bubble-blowing
      Imps! fill high the streams ye trouble,
      Till the bath be overflowing!

Come, old broom, be up and trudging!
  Take this ragged old apparel!
All thy life thou hast been drudging,
  And to serve me wilt not quarrel.
Head on two legs standing—
  What a funny creature!
Go, at my commanding
  With the water-pitcher!
      Boil and bubble!
      Water sources!
      Water courses!
      Bubble-blowing
      Imps! fill high the streams ye trouble,
      Till the bath be overflowing!

See, towards the shore he rushes;
  He is there! nor does he loiter;
Back with lightning speed! and gushes
  O'er the pitcher's brim the water!
Here again the creature!
  How the water's growing!
Every pail and pitcher
  Filled to overflowing!
      Hold, thou devil!
      More than measure
      For my pleasure
      Thou hast brought in!
      Ha! the spell-word—Woe and evil!
      Have I then the word forgotten?

Oh! the word wherewith my master
  Lays the spirits he has done with!
Ugh! he runs and brings the faster!
  Would the broom I'd not begun with!
Still those mad endeavours,
  Still fresh floods are pouring,
Till a hundred rivers
  Seem around me roaring!

No! no longer
I'll endure him;
I'll secure him!
This is malice!
Woe! ah woe! my fears grow stronger.
What a face! what features callous!

Wild thou, misbegotten devil!
  Drown the house with fiendish funning?
For the water o'er the level
  Of the sill in streams is running.
Just a broom-stick frantic,
  That will hear me never!
Be a stick, thou antic!
  Once more and for ever!
      Is unending
      This work dreary?
      Art not weary?
      Oh! remit it!
      Ah! this hatchet stops the offending,
      For the broom-stick, I will split it!

Here again, all dripping, dropping!
  Let me catch thee, thou uncouthness!
Now, O Kobold, for thy stopping!
  Crack and cleave, thou edge of smoothness!
Hit most excellently!
  He in twain is really!
Now incontinently
  Do I breathe more freely.
      Growing evils!
      Fearful wonder,
      As I sunder!
      For more showers
      Rush in air *two* menial devils!
      Help me! O ye heavenly Powers!

Down the stairs a cascade dashes,
  In the hall the flood's appalling!
Look, how horribly it splashes!
  Lord and master, hear me calling!
Ah! he comes! your revel
  Ends now, Imps of water.
Lord, I raised the devil,
  And I caught a Tartar!
      "In the corner,
      Broom! broom! quickly
      As a stick lie!
      Spirits all, you
      Hear your wizard and your warner—
      Never come until I call you!"

The Magician's Apprentice, an English verse translation by William Gibson (1886)
of *Der Zauberlehrling,* a ballad by Johann Wolfgang von Goethe (1797)

INSTRUMENTATION

Piccolo [Petite Flûte, P^{te} Fl.]
2 Flutes [Grandes Flûtes, G^{des} Fl.]
2 Oboes [Hautbois, Hautb., H^b]
2 Clarinets in B♭ [Clarinettes, Cl. (Si♭)]
Bass Clarinet in B♭ [Clarinette Basse, Cl. B. (Si♭)]
3 Bassoons [Bassons, B^{ons}]
Contrabassoon [Contrebasson, C. B^{on}]
  or Contrabass Sarrusophone

4 Horns in F [Cors (Fa)]
2 Trumpets in C [Tromp(ettes)(Ut)]
2 Cornets in B♭ [Cornets (à Pistons)(Si♭)]
3 Trombones [Tromb(ones)]

Timpani [Timbales, Timb.]

Harp [Harpe]

Percussion
  Glockenspiel [Glock(enspiel)]
   or Celesta
  Bass Drum [Grosse Caisse, G. C.]
  Cymbals [Cymbales, Cymb.]
  Triangle [Triangle, Trg.]

Violins 1, 2 [Violons]
Violas [Altos]
Cellos [Violoncelles, V^{elles}]
Basses [Contrebasses, C. B.]

Footnotes to the original score:
  The bass clarinet sounds a major 2nd lower than written.
  The trumpets must have mutes available.
  Each percussion instrument requires its own player.
  Cymbal rolls are played with timpani sticks on a cymbal suspended by its strap;
   bass drum rolls are played with a two-headed beater.

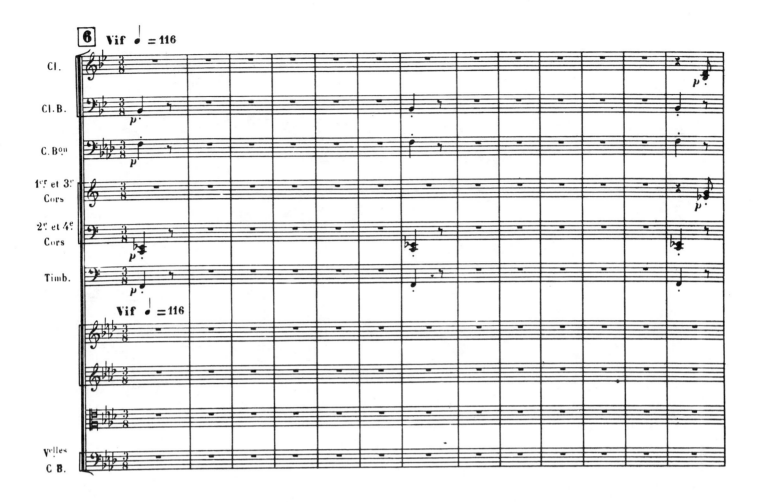

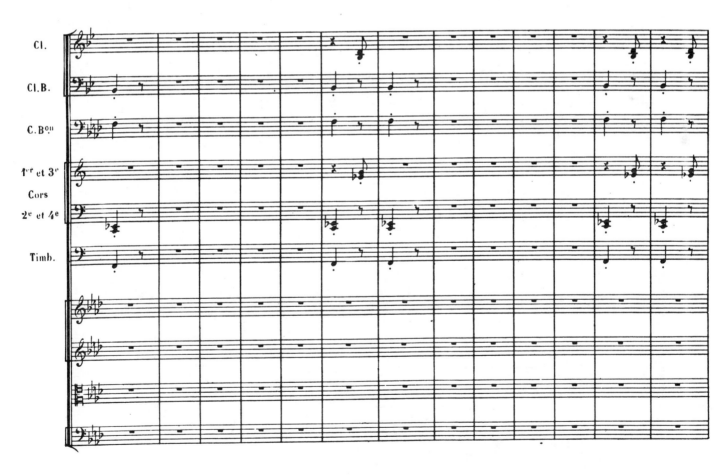

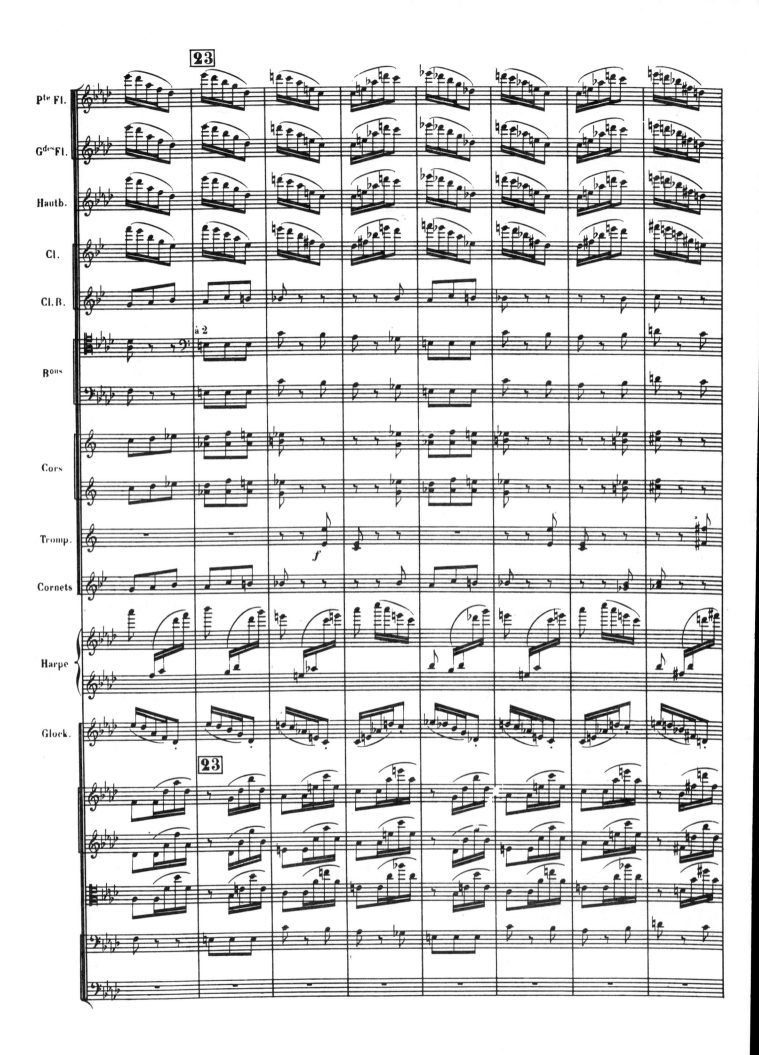

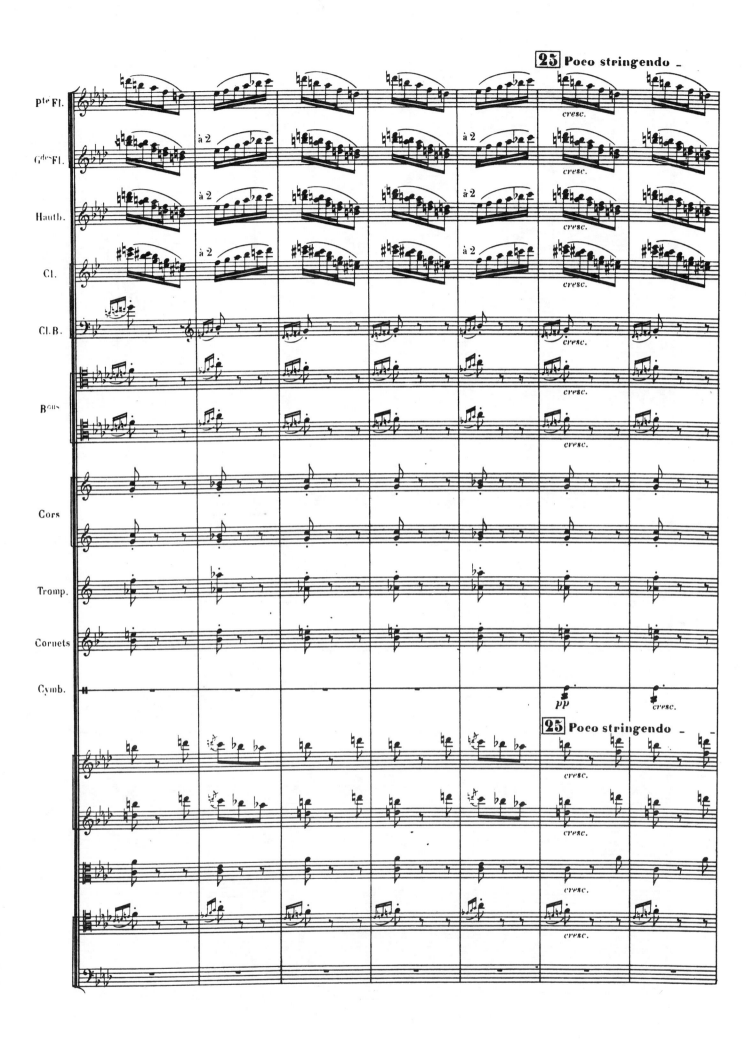

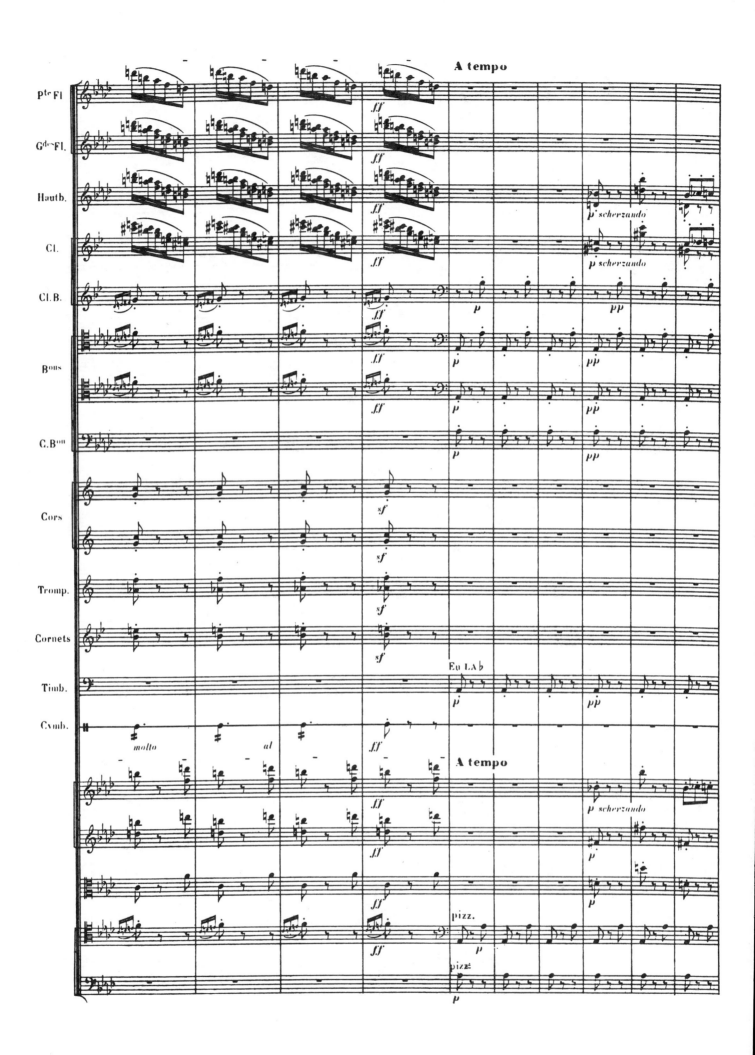

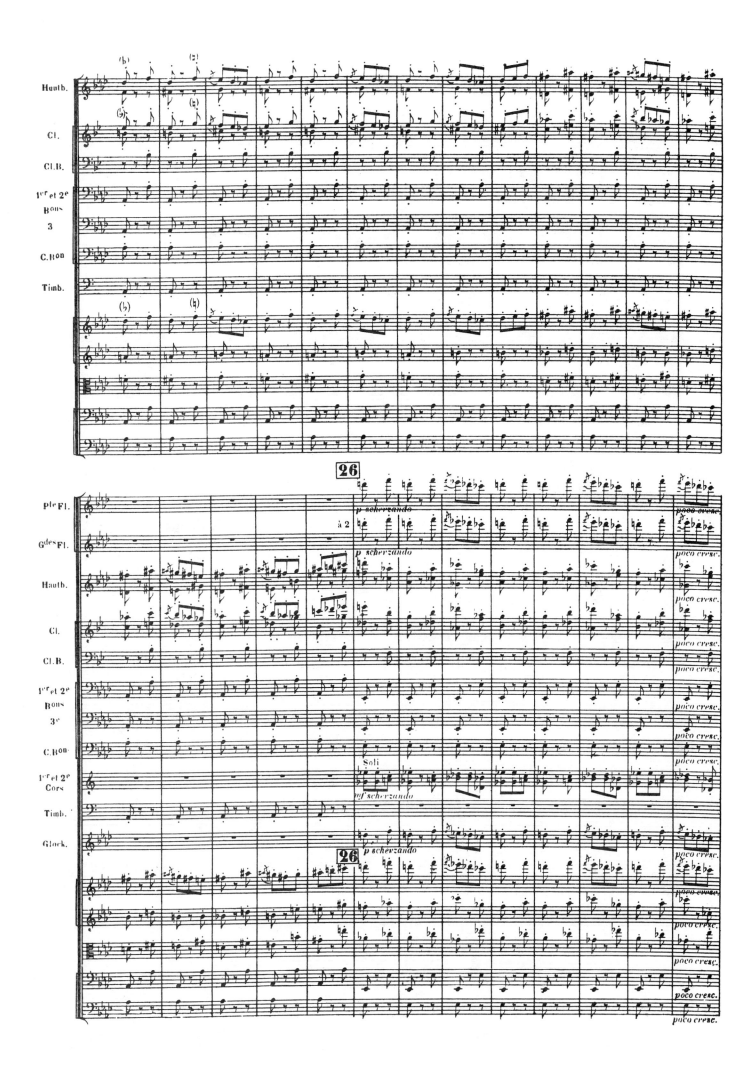

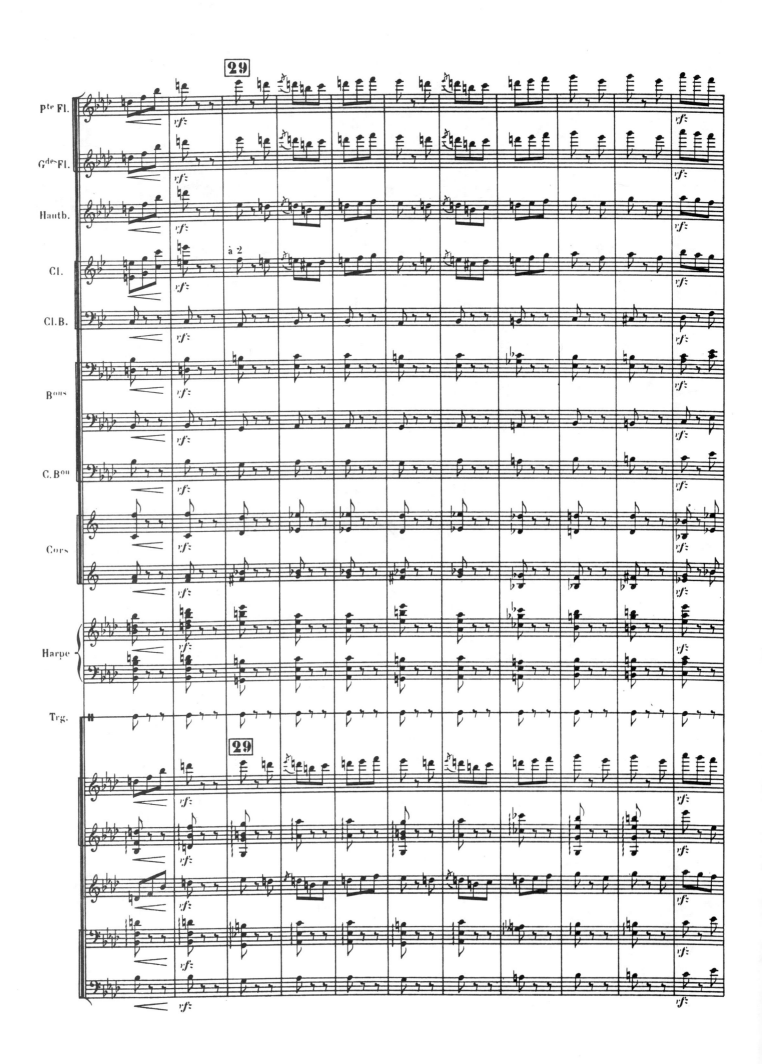

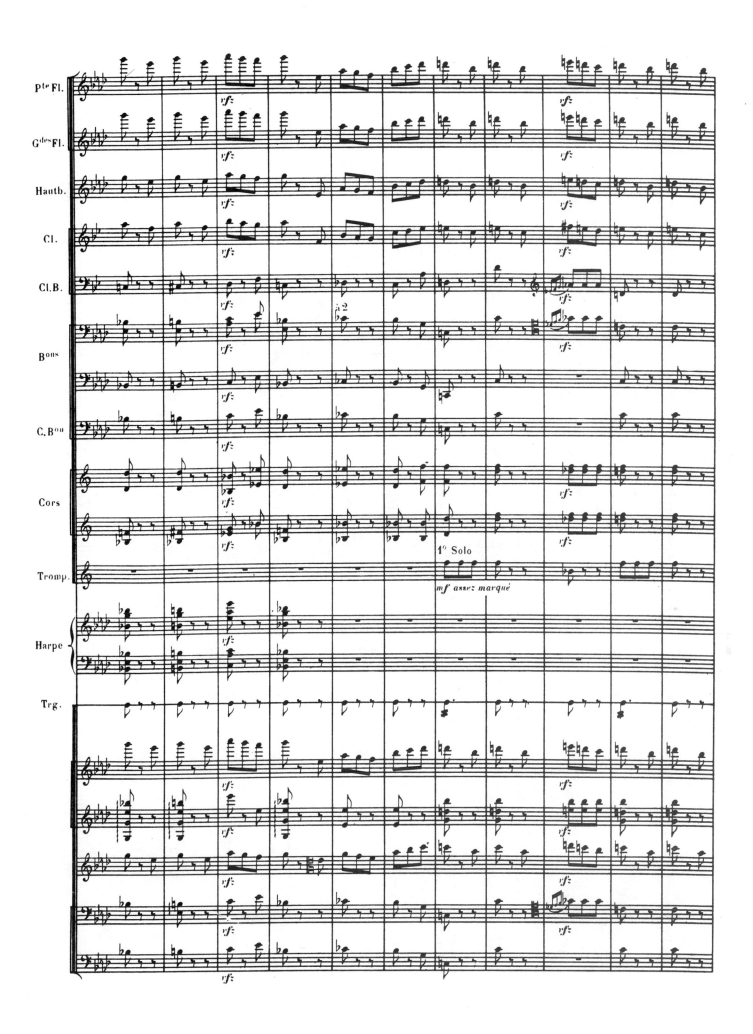

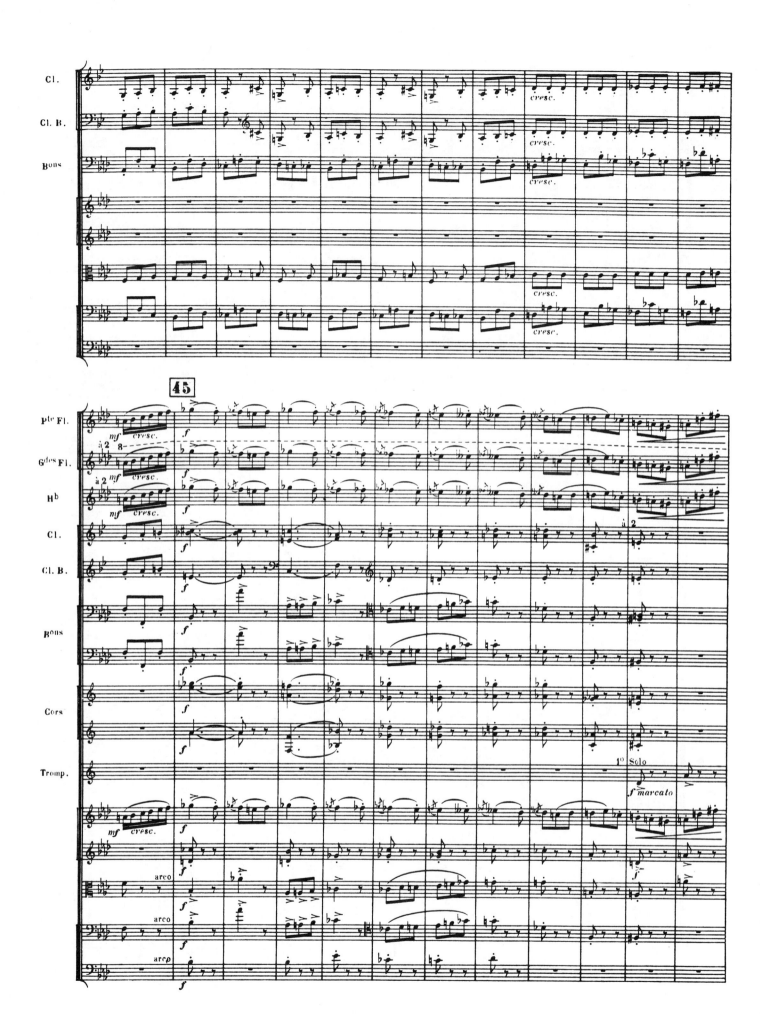

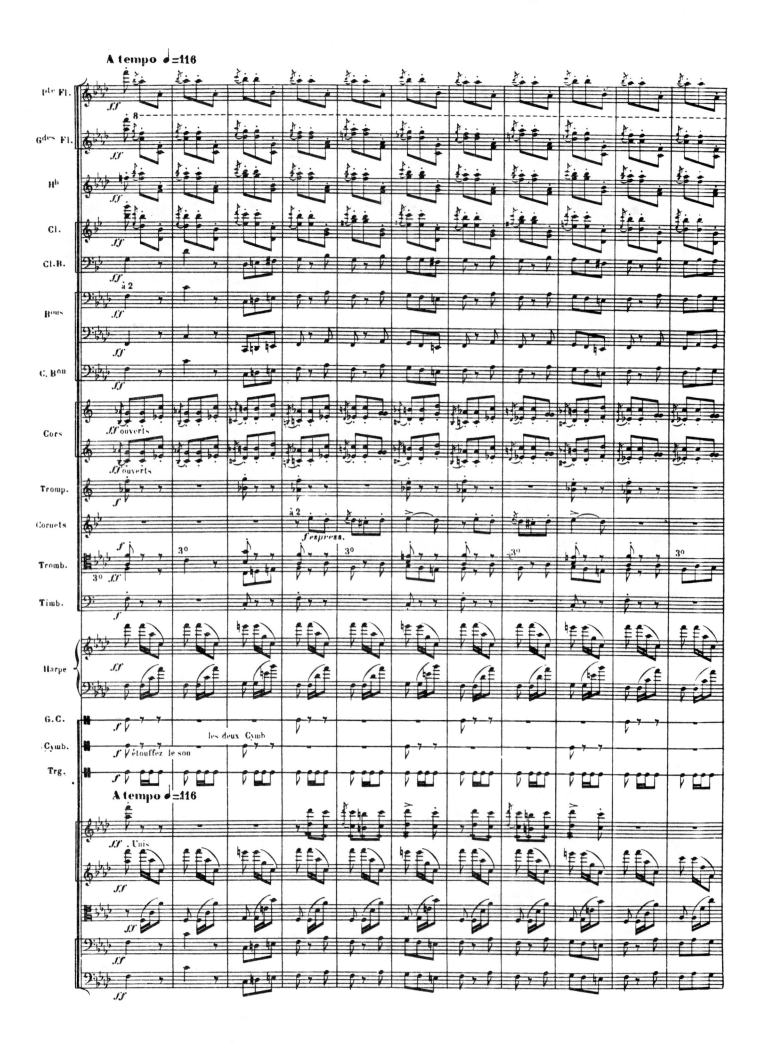

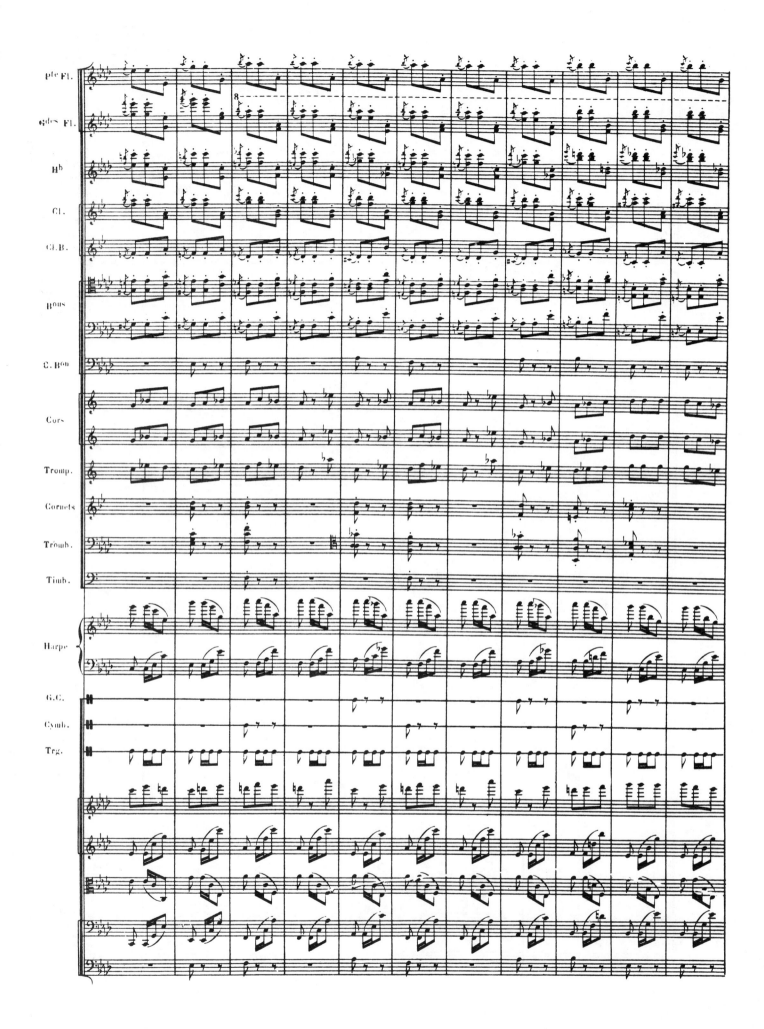

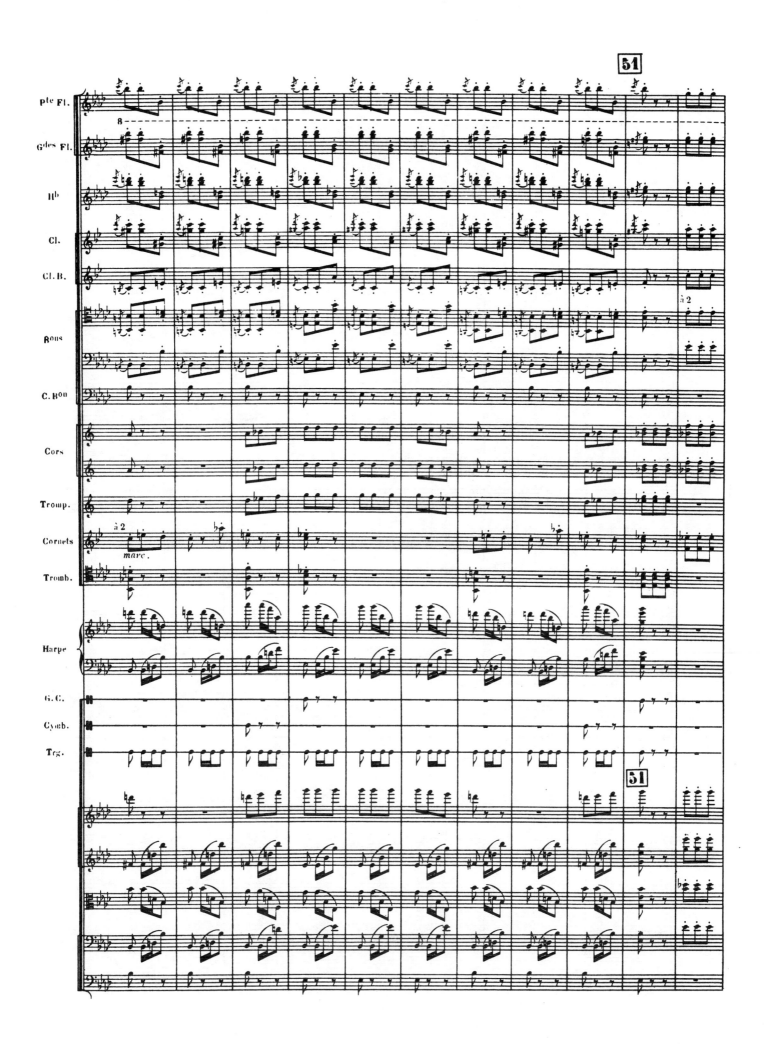

To Charles Lamoureux

Emmanuel Chabrier
ESPAÑA

Rhapsody for Orchestra

[Rapsodie pour orchestre]

(1883)

INSTRUMENTATION

Piccolo [Petite Flûte]
2 Flutes [Grandes Flûtes]
2 Oboes [Hautbois]
2 Clarinets in B♭ [Clarinettes (Si♭)]
4 Bassoons [Bassons]

4 Horns [Cors]: 2 in C (Ut)(*ordinaires*) /
    2 in F (Fa)(*chromatiques*)
2 Trumpets in F [Trompettes (*chromatiques*)(Fa)]
2 Cornets in B♭ [Pistons (Si♭)]
3 Trombones [Trombones]
Tuba [Tuba]

Timpani [Timbales]

2 Harps [Harpe]

Percussion
    Triangle [Triangle, Tr.]
    Tambourine [Tambour de Basque. T. de B.]
    Bass Drum & Cymbals [G^{sse} C^{sse}, Gr. C. et Cy(mb)]

Violins [Violons, V^{ons}]
Violas [Altos]
Cellos [Violoncelles]
Basses [Contrebasses]

mf e leggierissimo
mf
1º
mf leggierissimo
pp
sec.
dim
1º sec.
dimin.
poco a poco
p
Tr.
T. de B.
sempre pp
pizz.
f
dim.

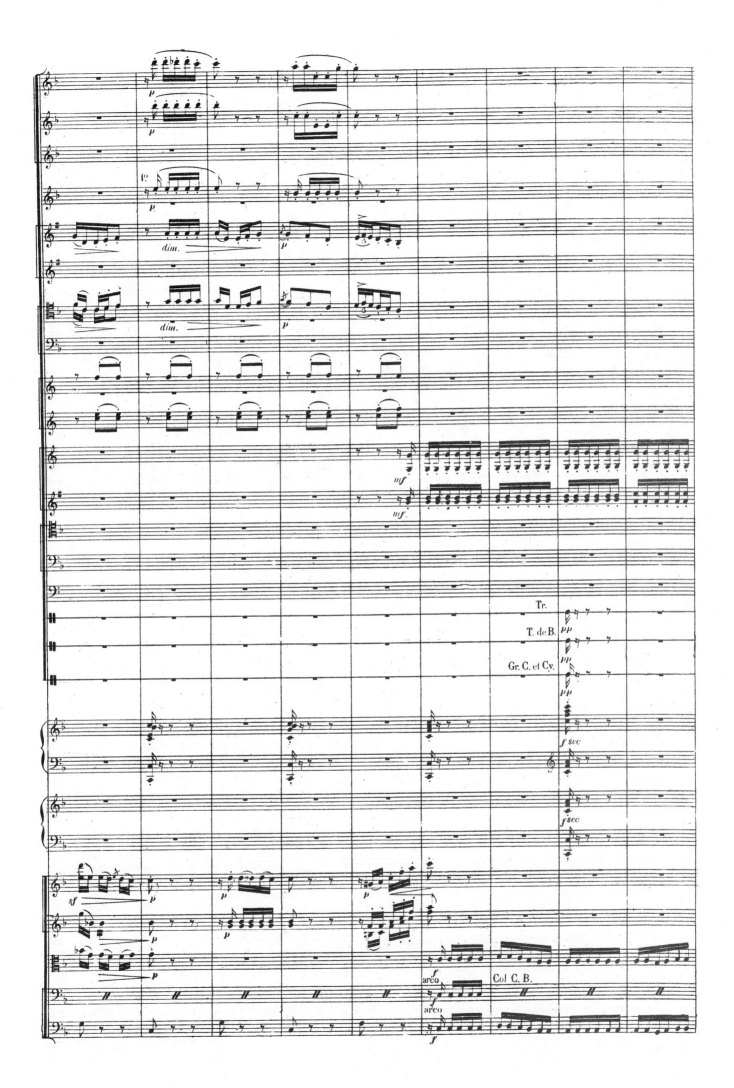

ff
ff
f
ff
ff
f e sempre cresc.
f e sempre cresc.
pp
pp
pp
cresc.
cresc.
cresc.
mf
mf
mf
4e Corde
4e Corde
3e Corde
f
f
cresc. sempre
cresc. sempre
cresc. sempre

END OF EDITION